# TROLL

# DINOSAURS
## AND OTHER PREHISTORIC ANIMALS

# TROLL
# DINOSAURS
## AND OTHER PREHISTORIC ANIMALS

by
Robin Wright
Illustrated by Don Wazejewski,
Ron Wardle, and Sol Kirby
Consultant: Tim Batty

**Troll Associates**

*Library of Congress Cataloging-in-Publication Data*

Wright, Robin, (date)
  Dinosaurs and other prehistoric animals / by Robin Wright;
illustrated by Don Wazejewski, Ron Wardle, and Sol Kirby.
    p.    cm.
  Summary: Describes the dinosaurs and other prehistoric reptiles,
examines individual species, and explains how paleontologists made
the fossil discoveries leading to our current knowledge.
  ISBN 0-8167-2232-3 (lib. bdg.)      ISBN 0-8167-2233-1 (pbk.)
  1. Dinosaurs—Juvenile literature.   2. Animals, Fossil—Juvenile
literature.  [1. Dinosaurs.  2. Prehistoric animals.
3. Paleontology.]  I. Wazejewski, Don, ill.  II. Wardle, Ron, ill.
III. Kirby, Sol, ill.  IV. Title.
QE862.D5W75  1991
567.9'1—dc20                                    90-38028

Published in the U.S.A. by Troll Associates, Inc.,
Produced for Troll Associates, Inc., by
Joshua Morris Publishing Inc. in association
with Harper Collins.
Printed in Belgium.
10 9 8 7 6 5 4 3 2 1

# Contents

# INTRODUCTION

Dinosaurs lived long ago. For millions of years, they roamed the earth. Then, mysteriously, they vanished. When they died, sand and mud covered their bodies. Over millions of years, the sand and mud turned to rock, and the dinosaur bones were preserved as fossils in it.

Scientists have divided dinosaurs into two main groups – saurischian (sore-ISS-kee-an) dinosaurs and ornithischian (or-nih-THISS-kee-an) dinosaurs. They are grouped like this

because of their hipbones. *Saurischian* means "lizard-hipped," and *ornithischian* means "bird-hipped."

This book tells you about some of these dinosaurs and about some other prehistoric animals. At the end of the book, there is a section on fossils and a list of museum displays in the United States where you can go and see for yourself what dinosaurs looked like.

# WHAT WERE THE DINOSAURS?

### "Terrible Lizards"

Long before there were any people, a large group of strange animals lived on earth. These animals were named dinosaurs – a word that means "terrible lizards." The dinosaurs were not really like lizards, though. They laid eggs and had scaly skins like lizards, but they differed enough from other reptiles to be in their own group. What really made them different from any other previous animals was the development of their hipbones.

The structure of these bones allowed them to walk on upright legs, while other reptiles walked with their legs spread out in an awkward position. The dinosaurs' improved stance gave them an advantage over other animals. They were able to run faster and support a far greater body weight.

Not all dinosaurs were large, though. Some were only the size of a chicken. There were hundreds of different types of dinosaurs. As a group, they were as varied as modern mammals. One thing they all had in common was that they were land animals.

*This shows the shape of a dinosaur's hip and leg bones (right), compared with those of a crocodile's or a lizard's (left). Because of this arrangement, many dinosaurs were able to stand upright.*

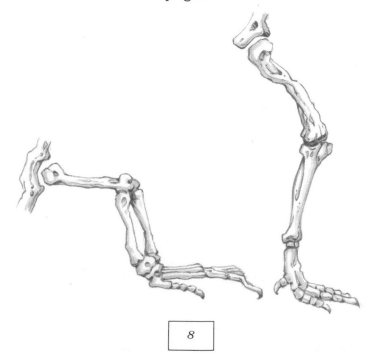

# RULERS OF THE LAND

The first dinosaurs appeared around 220 million years ago. For almost 150 million years, they ruled the land. The Age of Dinosaurs began around 245 million years ago and ended 66 million years ago. This stretch of time is called the Mesozoic (Mez-uh-ZOH-ik) Era. It is divided into three periods: the Triassic (Try-AS-ic) Period, the Jurassic (Jer-AS-ic) Period, and the Cretaceous (Kreh-TAY-shus) Period.

*Sizes of various dinosaurs in comparison to the size of a human being.*

# WHAT THE WORLD LOOKED LIKE

The maps on these pages show what the world looked like during the three periods of the Mesozoic Era and how the dinosaurs moved around the world.

## The Triassic Period

The world probably looked like this during the Triassic Period (245-208 million years ago). All the land areas were joined in a huge continent. Scientists call this continent Pangaea (Pan-JEE-ah). During the Triassic Period, the first dinosaurs were able to wander across the huge continent from one end to the other.

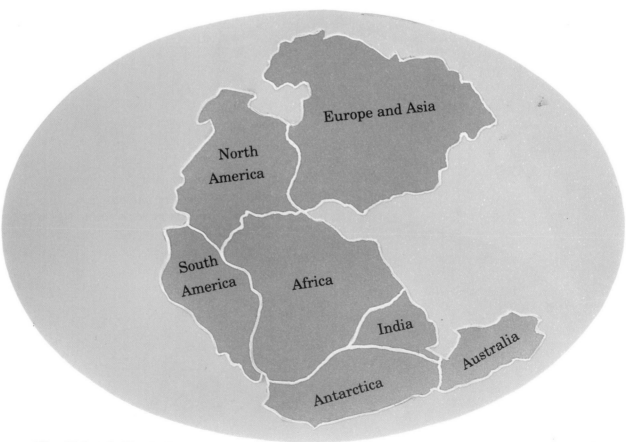

**The Triassic Period**

## The Jurassic Period

During the Jurassic Period (208-142 million years ago), Pangaea began to break up. The northern and southern continents were separating. But land bridges allowed the dinosaurs to spread to the north and south.

## The Cretaceous Period

In the Cretaceous Period (142-66 million years ago), oceans separated most of the land masses. This meant that dinosaurs could not travel across the world.

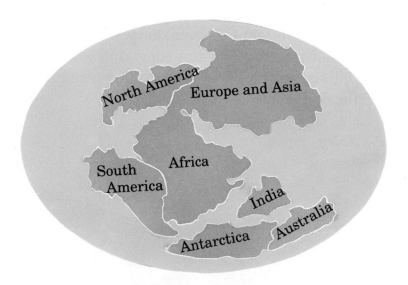

**The Jurassic Period**

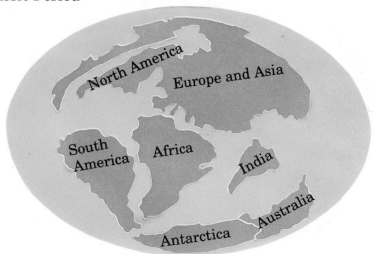

**The Cretaceous Period**

# WHAT THE WORLD WAS LIKE

## Climate and Environment

Between 245 and 208 million years ago, in the Triassic Period, the world was mostly desert.

It was during this period that the first dinosaurs developed from a group of early reptiles called thecodonts (THEE-koh-donts), meaning "socket-toothed." By the end of the Triassic Period, many of these reptiles were dying out, while more dinosaurs were appearing.

Tortoises and lizards shared the land with the early dinosaurs. In the air, some of the first flying reptiles, called pterosaurs (TER-uh-sorz), glided along on their leathery wings. Strange creatures, such as nothosaurs (NO-tho-sorz) and ichthyosaurs (IK-thee-uh-sorz), lived in the lakes and shallow seas from the middle of the Triassic Period.

*A pterosaur (top), an ichthyosaur (left), and a long-necked nothosaur (right) hunting for fish.*

During the Jurassic Period, 208-142 million years ago, the earth began to warm up. The climate became wetter and huge forests developed. The number and variety of dinosaurs increased. By the beginning of this period, the first flesh-eating dinosaurs had developed. And huge plant-eating dinosaurs walked the land in groups called herds. The number and variety of other animals and plants also increased during this time.

The world began to cool down during the Cretaceous Period, 142-66 million years ago. There were many more plants now, including the first flowering plants. The first deciduous (dih-SIJ-oo-us) trees – those that shed their leaves in winter – also developed and spread. It was during this period that many of our modern forms of animal and plant life developed.

## Life in the Air and Seas

One type of Cretaceous pterosaur, or flying lizard, was Quetzalcoatlus (Ket-sol-ko-AT-lus). This huge creature had a wingspan bigger than some fighter aircraft. Meanwhile, very large marine reptiles more than thirty-three feet (ten meters) long swam in the seas.

The close of the Cretaceous Period sixty-six million years ago was also the end of the Age of the Dinosaurs.

# WHERE THE DINOSAURS CAME FROM

Some scientists think dinosaurs can be traced back to a group of fish. A number of fish with lungs and stumpy fins developed into animals that could live both in the water and on the land. These are called amphibians.

From the water came the reptiles. These had scaly skins and laid waterproof eggs only on dry land.

*This chart shows the development of the dinosaurs.*

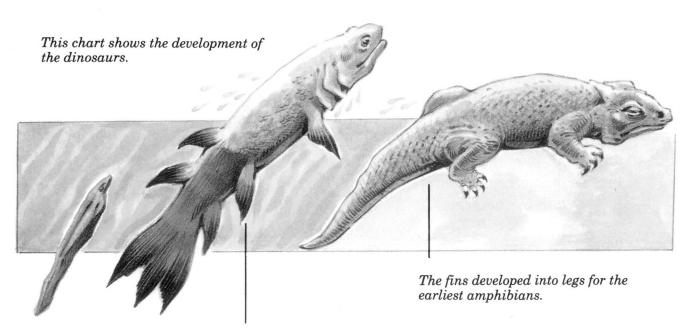

*The fins developed into legs for the earliest amphibians.*

*Lobe-finned fish, which breathed out of water, sometimes used their stumpy fins as legs.*

One group of reptiles was called the *archosaurs*, which means "ruling reptiles." Archosaurs had longer, straighter legs than the other reptiles. The dinosaurs belonged to this group. Other archosaurs were crocodiles and flying reptiles called pterosaurs. Pterosaurs were not dinosaurs, although they shared some similarities.

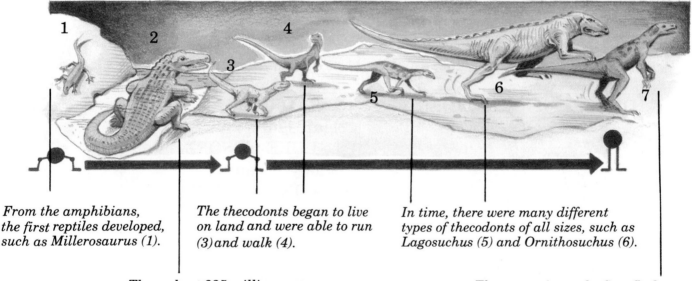

*From the amphibians, the first reptiles developed, such as Millerosaurus (1).*

*The thecodonts began to live on land and were able to run (3) and walk (4).*

*In time, there were many different types of thecodonts of all sizes, such as Lagosuchus (5) and Ornithosuchus (6).*

*Then, about 225 million years ago, the thecodonts developed. These included the proterosuchians ("earliest crocodiles") (2) who lived mainly in the water.*

*They gave rise to the first flesh-eating dinosaurs. Among them was Staurikosaurus (7).*

# HOW DINOSAURS ARE CLASSIFIED

There are two main groups, or orders, of dinosaurs, but each of these main groups is divided into smaller groups called suborders.

## Saurischian Dinosaurs

*Saurischian* means "lizard-hipped." These dinosaurs' hipbones were similar to those of other reptiles. There were two main types of saurischian dinosaurs: two-legged flesh-eaters called theropods (THER-uh-pods) and sauropodomorphs (sore-oh-POD-ah-morfs), the two- and four-legged plant-eaters. Scientists have divided these into several subgroups.

Theropods included lightweight coelurosaurs, swift and savage deinonychosaurs, and large-skulled, short-necked carnosaurs. Sauropodomorphs included two- and four-legged prosauropods and giant, four-legged sauropods.

This chart shows the classification of saurischian dinosaurs:

| ORDER | SUBORDER | INFRAORDER |
|---|---|---|
| saurischians | theropods | coelurosaurs (see-LURE-uh-SORZ) deinonychosaurs (dine-ON-ik-oh-SORZ) carnosaurs (KAR-nuh-SORZ) |
|  | sauropodomorphs | prosauropods (pro-SORE-uh-PODS) sauropods (SORE-oh-PODS) |

## Ornithischian Dinosaurs

*Ornithischian* means "bird-hipped." These dinosaurs had hip-bones like those of a bird. Some had bony beaks in front of their teeth.

There were four main types of ornithischian dinosaurs: two-legged ornithopods ("bird feet"), four-legged plated stegosaurs, horned ceratopsians, and armored ankylosaurs.

Ornithischian dinosaurs ate plants with their well-developed jaws. The teeth were set slightly back from the edge of the jaws. This allowed the fleshy cheeks to keep food from falling out while it was being chewed. The dinosaurs differed a great deal within the ornithischian order and were an extremely successful group, easily outnumbering the saurischians toward the end of the Age of the Dinosaurs.

This chart shows the classification of ornithischian dinosaurs:

| ORDER | SUBORDER |
|---|---|
| ornithischians | ornithopods (or-NITH-uh-pods)<br><br>stegosaurs  (STEG-uh-SORZ)<br><br>ankylosaurs  (ang-KILE-uh-SORZ)<br><br>ceratopsians (ser-uh-TOP-see-ahns) |

# DIFFERENT TYPES OF DINOSAURS

Dinosaurs did not all live at the same time. Many dinosaurs were the ancestors of others. Look at these lists to see which dinosaurs lived during each part of the Age of Dinosaurs. You'll read about many of these dinosaurs on the pages following the lists.

## Late Triassic Period / Early Jurassic Period
## 220-180 million years ago

Anchisaurus
Coelophysis
Euskelosaurus
Heterodontosaurus
Lesothosaurus
Plateosaurus
Scelidosaurus
Teratosaurus
Thecodontosaurus

*Teratosaurus*

*Plateosaurus*

*Anchisaurus*

## Middle Jurassic Period
## 180-160 million years ago

Lexovisaurus
Megalosaurus

*Megalosaurus*

*Lexovisaurus*

## Late Jurassic Period
## 160-142 million years ago

Allosaurus
Apatosaurus
Atlantosaurus
Barosaurus
Brachiosaurus
Camarasaurus
Ceratosaurus
Chialingosaurus
Coelurus
Compsognathus
Diplodocus
Kentrosaurus
Stegosaurus
Supersaurus

*Stegosaurus*

## Early Cretaceous Period
## 142-100 million years ago

Camptosaurus
Deinonychus
Hypsilophodon
Iguanodon
Polacanthus
Sauropelta
Yaverlandia

*Hypsilophodon*

## Late Cretaceous Period
## 100-66 million years ago

Alamosaurus
Albertosaurus
Ankylosaurus
Corythosaurus
Dromaeosaurus
Dromiceiomimus
Dryptosaurus
Euoplocephalus
Hypacrosaurus
Lambeosaurus
Monoclonius

*Euoplocephalus*

*Scolosaurus*

*Euoplocephalus (top) and Scolosaurus (bottom) are now considered to be the same dinosaur by many experts.*

Ornithomimus
Pachycephalosaurus
Panoplosaurus
Parasaurolophus
Protoceratops
Saurolophus
Spinosaurus
Stegoceras
Triceratops
Tyrannosaurus

*Triceratops*

# SAURISCHIAN DINOSAURS
## Theropods

Theropods, or "beast feet," were a group of flesh-eating saurischian dinosaurs. Scientists believe that only around ten percent of all dinosaurs were flesh-eaters.

The three main infraorders of theropods are carnosaurs, deinonychosaurs, and coelurosaurs.

*The carnosaur Allosaurus attacking a Camarasaurus.*

# CARNOSAURS

Carnosaurs, or "flesh lizards," were a group of very large flesh-eating dinosaurs. They preyed on plant-eaters. Their big, sharp teeth were their best weapons. These teeth were saw-edged, like a steak knife. Carnosaurs also had large, curved claws.

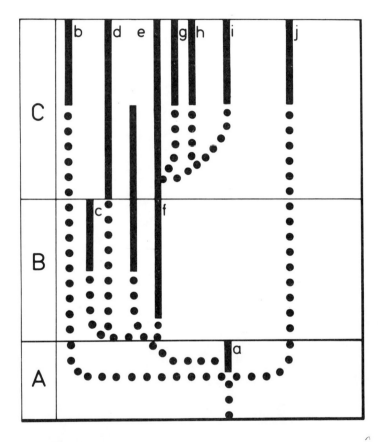

**Carnosaur family tree**

This family tree shows the ten carnosaur families. The dots show how they may be related to each other.

**a** teratosaurids
**b** therizinosaurids
**c** ceratosaurids
**d** spinosaurids
**e** allosaurids
**f** megalosaurids
**g** dryptosaurids
**h** tyrannosaurids
**i** itemirids
**j** segnosaurids
**A** Triassic Period
**B** Jurassic Period
**C** Cretaceous Period

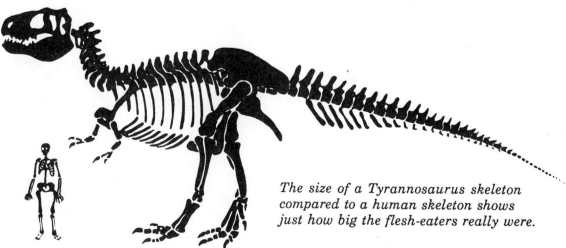

*The size of a Tyrannosaurus skeleton compared to a human skeleton shows just how big the flesh-eaters really were.*

## Megalosaurus (MEG-uh-loh-SORE-us)

Megalosaurus ("great lizard") was a big, heavy-bodied carnosaur with curved, saw-edged teeth. It had strong, curved claws on its toes and fingers. These Jurassic creatures grew to thirty feet (nine meters) and may have weighed as much as two tons (over one and a half metric tons).

*Megalosaurus*

**Allosaurus** (Al-uh-SORE-us)

Allosaurus ("other lizard") was like Megalosaurus, only larger. Living in the Jurassic Period, this creature has been called "the tiger of its age." It was about as long as a bus and weighed two tons. One monster found in North America may have been forty-two feet (thirteen meters) long and possibly weighed four tons (about three and a half metric tons). Fossilized tracks show that this predator may have been able to chase and attack a sauropod forty times heavier than itself. But to bring down a huge plant-eater such as Apatosaurus (Ah-PAT-uh-SORE-us), a whole group of Allosaurus probably would have been needed.

*Allosaurus*

## Ceratosaurus (Ser-AT-oh-SORE-us)

This "horned lizard" was an inhabitant of North America about 130 million years ago. It was over twenty feet (six meters) long and eight feet (two and a half meters) high. It was like an Allosaurus except for the short horn on its nose and the four-fingered hands.

*Ceratosaurus*

## Dryptosaurus (DRIP-tuh-SORE-us)

When Dryptosaurus was discovered in 1866, it was thought that this Late Cretaceous creature used its huge hind legs to leap onto the back of its prey. The name means "wounding lizard," referring to the belief that the animal wounded its victims by striking them with its eaglelike claws. The original name for Dryptosaurus was Laelaps (LYE-laps). Some scientists think that Dryptosaurus fossils found throughout North America may really belong to different Late Cretaceous dinosaurs.

*Dryptosaurus*

## Spinosaurus (SPY-nuh-SORE-us)

This strange creature had six-foot-long (two-meter-long) spines growing out of its back. These probably supported a large fleshy "sail." It is possible that the animal used its "sail" as a way of regulating its body temperature. By turning at right angles to the sun when the weather was cold, it could absorb heat and warm up. An overheated Spinosaurus might have turned its back on the sun to shed unwanted heat.

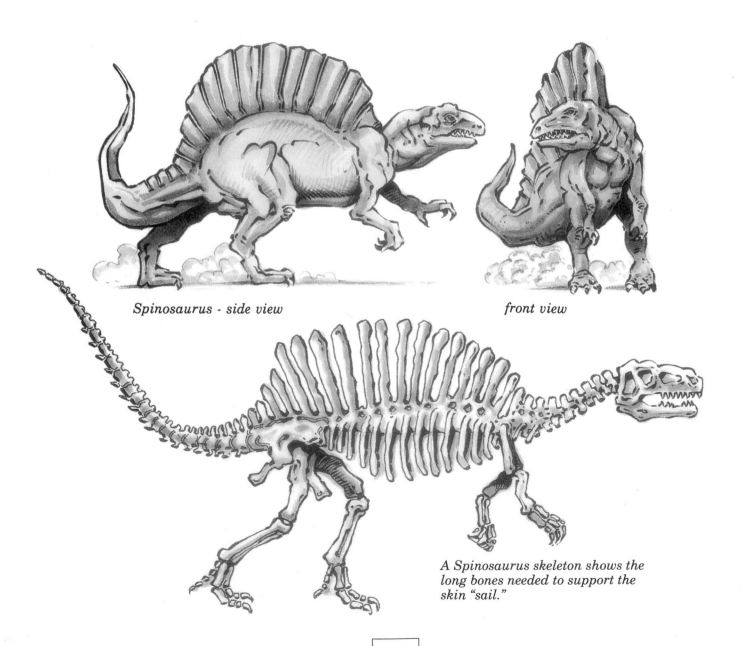

*Spinosaurus - side view*

*front view*

*A Spinosaurus skeleton shows the long bones needed to support the skin "sail."*

Spinosaurus ("spiny lizard") was about forty feet (about twelve meters) long and weighed seven tons (about six and a half metric tons). It lived in Egypt and Niger during the Late Cretaceous Period. Whether Spinosaurus walked on two or four legs is still debated by some scientists.

*Spinosaurus*

## Tyrannosaurus (Tie-RAN-uh-SORE-us)

Tyrannosaurus, or "tyrant lizard," was one of the largest flesh-eating animals of all time. It had huge, saw-edged teeth up to seven inches (eighteen centimeters) long and weighed as much as some elephants.

Scientists believe this Late Cretaceous dinosaur was fifty feet (fifteen meters) long and towered more than eighteen feet (five and a half meters) high. This monster weighed up to seven tons (six and a half metric tons).

*A Tyrannosaurus skull. It was light for its size because of the hollow spaces inside it.*

Though the carnosaurs have a reputation for being the fiercest animals of their time, not all scientists agree. Some experts think that their large size would have made it difficult to run for long distances to chase down prey. When they could not catch smaller, speedier creatures, the carnosaurs may have been part-time scavengers.

*Carnosaurs may have ambushed their prey, attacking in a short burst of speed.*

## DEINONYCHOSAURS

This was a group of medium-sized flesh-eaters. Scientists believe that they were among the fastest hunters of all time. Apart from their sharp teeth, they had a huge, sickle-shaped claw on each foot.

## Deinonychus (Dine-ON-ik-us)

In 1964, Professor John Ostrom of Yale University unearthed the remains of what turned out to be one of the fastest, fiercest, most agile hunters of any age. He later named it Deinonychus, which means "terrible claw." This fearsome creature was only about ten feet (three meters) long and lightly built, but it had a vicious sickle-shaped claw on each foot. There were also three hooked claws on each hand. These claws were used for grasping and tearing its prey.

*Deinonychus*

Deinonychus may have hunted in packs, often ambushing their victims. Working as a group, they were capable of bringing down Cretaceous dinosaurs much larger than themselves.

**Dromaeosaurus** (Drom-ee-uh-SORE-us)
Dromaeosaurus ("running lizard") was another type of deinonychosaur. This was a human-sized predator, even smaller than Deinonychus. It was about six feet (nearly two meters) long.

*Scientists think that deinonychosaurs may have hunted in packs.*

## COELUROSAURS

Another group of flesh-eating dinosaurs was the coelurosaurs, or "hollow-tailed lizards," a name given to them because they had hollow bones like a bird's. Coelurosaurs were among the smartest of dinosaurs and existed through most of the Mesozoic Era.

One family of coelurosaurs was the ornithomimids (or-NITH-oh-MY-mids). The name means "bird imitators." They looked like some modern flightless birds, such as the ostrich and emu.

*Ornithomimus*

These ostrichlike dinosaurs could sprint very quickly on their long, slim legs. In fact, they were probably the fastest dinosaurs of all. Lightweight coelurosaurs of the Cretaceous Period could have easily outrun the fastest human.

**Dromiceiomimus** (Dro-miss-ee-oh-MY-mus)
These creatures grew up to eleven feet (three and a half meters) in length and weighed about 220 pounds (100 kilograms). They were among the brainiest and speediest of all dinosaurs.

*Although they lived millions of years apart, Dromiceiomimus could probably run as fast as a modern horse.*

# Sauropodomorphs

The word *sauropodomorph* means "lizard-footed forms." These saurischian dinosaurs had small heads and long tails and necks. There were two different infraorders of sauropodomorphs: sauropods and prosauropods.

Sauropods were the largest dinosaurs – and the largest land animals – that have ever lived. They were often longer than today's largest buses. Fossils of a sauropod found in Colorado show that some of these creatures may have grown to more than 100 feet (21 meters) long.

The body of a sauropod was huge and heavy, at times weighing more than a dozen elephants combined. Each sauropod had four legs as large as tree trunks to support its great weight. The brains of sauropods, however, were small in relation to the size of their bodies.

From the fossil remains of sauropod jaws, scientists know that these creatures ate only plants. Even though they were gigantic, they were harmless to other animals. They probably had the same habits as elephants do today, spending most of their time grazing peacefully. Their sheer size would have helped to protect them from their enemies.

## SAUROPODS

There were five main groups of sauropods: camarasaurs (KAM-uh-ruh-sorz), cetiosaurs (SEET-ee-oh-sorz), brachiosaurs (BRAK-ee-uh-sorz), diplodocids (dih-PLOD-uh-kids), and titanosaurs (tie-TAN-uh-sorz).

### Camarasaurs

Camarasaurs were named after the dinosaur called Camarasaurus (KAM-uh-ruh-SORE-us), meaning "chambered lizard." This is because they had chambers, or hollow spaces, in their backbones. Camarasaurus was thirty to sixty feet (nine to eighteen meters) long.

### Cetiosaurs

Cetiosaurs were named after the dinosaur called Cetiosaurus (SEET-ee-oh-SORE-us), which measured about forty-five feet (about fourteen meters) long – as long as eight tall humans laid end to end.

### Brachiosaurs

This group of dinosaurs took its name from one of the largest and heaviest of all dinosaurs: Brachiosaurus ("arm lizard"). Its front legs were longer than its hind legs. Some of these animals weighed up to ninety tons (eighty-two metric tons) or more than 1,400 people of average weight put together.

The fossilized remains of an even larger brachiosaur were found in western Colorado in 1972. The dinosaur was called Supersaurus (SOO-per-SORE-us). Supersaurus may have weighed over 100 tons (91 metric tons). Since this discovery, scientists have found two other dinosaurs that may have weighed even more than Supersaurus.

## Diplodocids

These sauropods had nostrils high on their heads, and weak teeth. The diplodocid known as Atlantosaurus (At-lan-tuh-SORE-us) measured around seventy-five feet (twenty-three meters) from head to tail. Another member of the group was Diplodocus. The name means "double beam," after the shape of its middle tail bones. These bones had double skids to protect the blood vessels if the tail dragged on the ground. Diplodocus grew up to ninety feet (twenty-seven meters) long. Another diplodocid of similar length was Barosaurus (Bar-uh-SORE-us), though it had a longer neck and a shorter tail.

## Titanosaurs

Their name means "large lizards." Titanosaurs were named after Titanosaurus (Tie-TAN-uh-SORE-us). This sauropod was sixty to sixty-six feet (eighteen to twenty meters) long and may have had armor plates. Its fossils have been found in India, Europe, Africa, Mongolia, and South America.

*Diplodocids*

## PROSAUROPODS

Most scientists think prosauropods, meaning "before lizard feet," were the ancestors of the big, four-legged, plant-eating dinosaurs. They lived from Middle Triassic to Early Jurassic times, when they gradually spread throughout the world.

Prosauropods varied in size. Some, like Anchisaurus (ANG-kee-SORE-us), were only about eight feet (two and a half meters) long. Others, such as Euskelosaurus (You-SKEL-uh-SORE-us), grew up to forty feet (over twelve meters) and weighed two tons (nearly two metric tons).

*Anchisaurus - eight feet (two and a half meters) long*

*Euskelosaurus - forty feet (twelve meters) long*

Plateosaurus (PLAY-tee-uh-SORE-us), a prosauropod that was one of the first big dinosaurs, was about twenty-six feet (eight meters) long. It moved on all four feet, but it could balance on its hind legs. This would have helped it reach the tops of trees for food. Another prosauropod, Massospondylus (Mass-o-SPON-dih-lus), may have had stones in its stomach to help it grind and digest the plants it ate.

The prosauropods died out quite early in the Jurassic Period. However, the sauropods who came after them lived through the Jurassic Period and into the Cretaceous Period.

*Plateosaurus - twenty-six feet (eight meters) long*

*Massospondylus - thirteen feet (four meters) long*

# BENEFITS OF BEING BIG

Being big had several advantages for the sauropods. They were too large to be badly hurt by most of the meat-eaters, especially one against one. The long necks of the sauropods helped them spot danger early, such as an approaching pack of meat-eaters. And they could have used their long, heavy tails to ward off attackers.

Sauropods certainly had very healthy appetites. Scientists believe that a large sauropod ate half a ton (508 kilograms) of plant matter every day.

Despite their size, few of these lumbering creatures survived beyond the Middle Cretaceous Period, and none left any descendants. It could be that while size protected the adults, the small youngsters were easy prey to many of the meat-eaters. However, scientists believe that the youngsters were probably given some protection by the adults in the group.

*Sauropod defending itself against a smaller meat-eater.*

## Land or Water Animals?

Because sauropods had weak teeth, some scientists used to think that they grazed only on soft water plants. It was thought that these gigantic animals must have spent their life buoyed up by water since they were too heavy to have stood up on dry land. It was also thought that their long necks helped them breathe as they waded in deep lakes.

The tracks some sauropods left behind seem to show that they spent part of their time wading in water. However, if they had stayed in deep water all the time, water pressure would have been too great for their lungs to expand for breathing. Now scientists know that the sauropods' massive legs could bear their weight on land. It seems likely that they roamed around in herds like monstrous elephants. They probably used their long necks to reach high treetop leaves, just as giraffes do today.

*Sauropods feeding.*

# ORNITHISCHIAN DINOSAURS
# Ornithopods

The name *ornithopod* means "bird-footed," after their foot bones, which were like those of a bird.

Ornithopods were the only ornithischian dinosaurs that were able to walk and run on their hind legs. They varied from the size of a dog to that of an elephant.

**Heterodontosaurus** (Het-er-uh-DON-tuh-SORE-us)
One of these early ornithischian dinosaurs was Heterodontosaurus. Its name means "lizard with different teeth." This Triassic creature had some sharp cutting teeth, fangs behind those, and other teeth with flattened tops–more like a mammal's than a reptile's. It also had cheek pouches to store its food as it chewed. Most of these plant-eaters were only about four feet (over a meter) long and were found in what is now Africa.

**Lesothosaurus** (Leh-SOTH-uh-SORE-us)
Lesothosaurus was another early ornithopod. This three-foot-long (just under a meter long) dinosaur had sharp teeth, and its lower jaw ended in a horny beak. This helped it chop off leaves and twigs.

Lesothosaurus

## Hypsilophodonts (Hip-sih-LO-fuh-donts)

Hypsilophodonts were a family of larger bird-footed dinosaurs.
These were slim, speedy, and probably able to sprint and leap as
nimbly as a gazelle of today. They grew up to twenty feet (six
meters) in length, although most were much smaller.

*Hypsilophodon*

## Iguanodon (Ih-GWAH-no-DON)

Another descendant of the smaller bird-hipped dinosaurs was the
gigantic Iguanodon. This creature was almost as heavy as an
elephant and could rear up as high as a second-story window.
The Iguanodon was about sixteen feet (five meters) tall. It was
nearly thirty feet (nine meters) long and weighed up to five tons
(four and a half metric tons).

*Iguanodon*

# BONEHEADED ORNITHOPODS: PACHYCEPHALOSAURS

A strange new group of bird-hipped dinosaurs developed in the late Cretaceous Period, about eighty million years ago. They were called pachycephalosaurs (pak-ee-SEF-uh-lo-sorz), which means "boneheaded lizards."

## Yaverlandia (Yah-ver-LAND-ee-ah)

The first boneheaded dinosaur was Yaverlandia. This was a small, turkey-sized dinosaur. It had a long, stiff tail and bony bumps around its eyes. It lived in what is now the south of England.

## Stegoceras (Steg-OSS-air-us)

Stegoceras, or "horny roof," was a human-sized bonehead. Its brain was only the size of a hen's egg, although its skull was five times thicker than a human's. Stegoceras lived in North America and possibly in China.

*Yaverlandia three feet (ninety centimeters) long*

*Stegoceras - six and a half feet (two meters) long*

## Pachycephalosaurus (Pak-ee-SEF-uh-lo-SORE-us)

Pachycephalosaurus, or "thick-headed lizard," was the largest boneheaded dinosaur. It had the thickest, spikiest skull of all–about ten inches (twenty-five centimeters) thick. Bony knobs further reinforced the back and front of the skull. At first, scientists thought that this strange skull shape had been caused by a disease. Now they think that the thick skulls worked like crash helmets, protecting the brains of rival males who butted each other to win the attention of females. This is similar to the mating practices of deer and caribou.

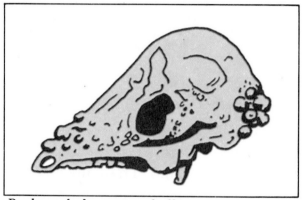

*Pachycephalosaurus skull*

## DUCK-BILLED ORNITHOPODS: HADROSAURS

Hadrosaurs (HAD-ruh-sorz), or "duck-billed lizards," were among the last and most successful of all the dinosaurs. They got the name "duckbill" from their broad, toothless beaks. Scientists have found large quantities of hadrosaur remains. They believe these dinosaurs were among the most varied, abundant groups of dinosaurs.

Hadrosaurs were similar to Iguanodons. Some of them grew to over thirty feet (nine meters) long and weighed up to three tons (about three metric tons). Their jaws held rows of grinding teeth. Some species had as many as 2,000 teeth. As old ones fell out, new ones grew. The rich supply of grinding teeth helped duckbills chew all kinds of tough plants and pine needles. The fossilized remains of these foods were actually found in the body of one long-dead hadrosaur.

*Hadrosaur compared to a human being.*

## Mysterious Crests

The strangest thing about some duckbills was the bony crest on their heads. These differently shaped head ornaments probably helped one type of duckbill to recognize others of the same species. Any other use remains a mystery. They would have been little use in protecting the animals. It is possible that the crests improved their sense of smell, helping them to avoid enemies. It has also been suggested that the hollow crests were used to amplify (make louder) warning signals and mating calls.

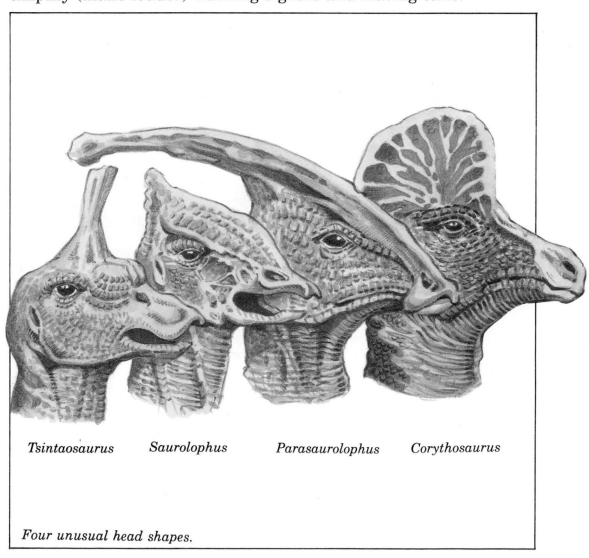

*Tsintaosaurus*      *Saurolophus*      *Parasaurolophus*      *Corythosaurus*

*Four unusual head shapes.*

# Stegosaurs

The name *Stegosaurs* means "plated lizards." These ornithischians were known as *plated* dinosaurs because of the plates and spikes on their backs and tails.

**Stegosaurus** (Steg-oh-SORE-us)

This very odd-looking dinosaur lived in North America about 150 million years ago. Its name means "plated lizard," after the many plates and spines along its back. The largest plate was nearly thirty inches (seventy-six centimeters) tall and thirty-one inches (seventy-nine centimeters) wide. Each plate was about two inches (five centimeters) thick and was covered with tough skin. Scientists are not sure exactly how the plates were arranged. It is likely, however, that the plates alternated in a zigzag pattern.

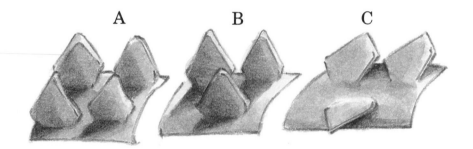

*Three possible arrangements of Stegosaurus's big, bony plates.*
*A. Paired upright  B. Alternating upright  C. Flopped outward*

*An arrangement like this could have helped regulate body temperature.*

Scientists are not certain about the purpose of the plates. They might have been used like a radiator to regulate body temperature. Stegosaurus also may have swung its spiky tail like a huge club to drive off carnosaurs. This huge creature may have grown as large as thirty feet (nine meters) in length and weighed up to two tons (nearly two metric tons).

Despite its great size, Stegosaurus had a head only sixteen inches (forty-one centimeters) long, with a brain the size of a walnut.

*Stegosaurus*

## Bumps and Spikes

Creatures such as Stegosaurus roamed the lush forests of North America and Europe 150 million years ago. Before then, the armor on dinosaurs was less spectacular but probably just as effective.

### Scelidosaurus (Skel-EE-doh-SORE-us)

The first known plated dinosaur was Scelidosaurus, which lived in what is now the south of England 190 million years ago. Rows of bony studs along its back protected it from the teeth of meat-eaters.

There is disagreement among scientists as to whether Scelidosaurus is an early stegosaur, an ankylosaur, or even an ornithopod (bird-footed dinosaur).

*Scelidosaurus*

### Chialingosaurus (Chye-ah-ling-uh-SORE-us)

A later stegosaur was Chialingosaurus, named after the Chialing River in China where its remains were found. This was a slim, thirteen-foot-long (four-meter-long) creature with small spiny plates.

*Chialingosaurus*

## Lexovisaurus (Lex-OH-vuh-SORE-us)

Lexovisaurus was a plated dinosaur that lived in Europe during the middle of the Jurassic Period. This was probably the ancestor of several different kinds of spiny dinosaurs.

*Lexovisaurus*

## Kentrosaurus (KEN-truh-SORE-us)

Among the spiniest of all was Kentrosaurus, "pointed lizard," which may have reached seventeen feet (five meters) in length. As its name suggests, it had pointed triangular plates on its back, arranged in pairs, and long spikes on its tail.

Although the tails and backs of plated dinosaurs were well protected, these animals were slow moving. As they lumbered around to face an enemy or reared up in defense, their sides and unprotected bellies were vulnerable. Still, stegosaurs as a group survived for more than fifty million years.

*Kentrosaurus*

# Ankylosaurs

The name *ankylosaurs* means "armored lizards." These armored dinosaurs developed after the plated dinosaurs. Ankylosaurs were far better able to cope with flesh-eaters. Their bodies were so low that they could drop quickly to the ground when danger threatened. Some scientists think that a few armored dinosaurs could roll themselves up in a ball, as armadillos do today.

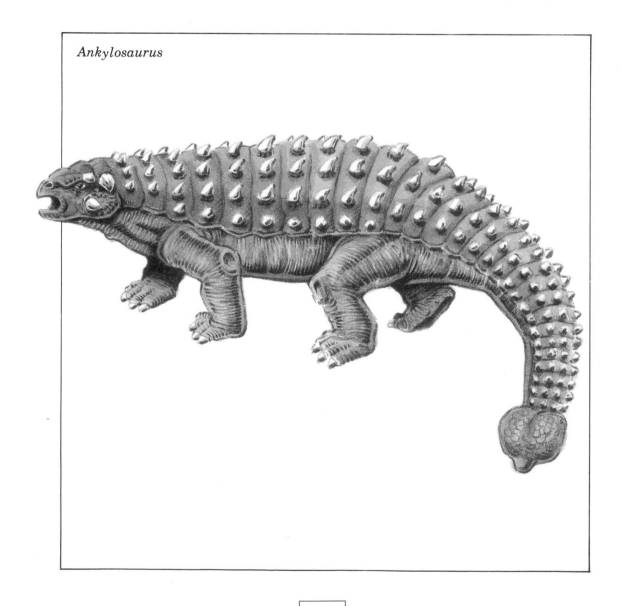

*Ankylosaurus*

## Euoplocephalus (You-OP-luh-SEF-uh-lus)

This was a North American ankylosaur and among the best protected. A blanket of bony plates covered its back from head to tail. The tail ended in a massive bony club. Euoplocephalus weighed about three tons (over two and a half metric tons) and was the size of a military tank.

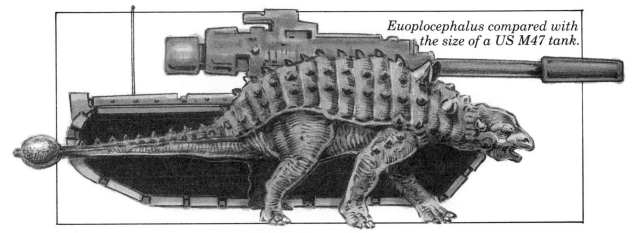

*Euoplocephalus compared with the size of a US M47 tank.*

## Sauropelta (Sore-uh-PEL-tah)

Sauropelta ("lizard shield") was another North American dinosaur. It had a long, narrow skull, with bands of small and large shields across its back. Spines may also have stuck out from its sides. Sauropelta was certainly one of the largest ankylosaurs. One found in Montana was twenty-five feet (about seven and a half meters) long and weighed three and a half tons (just over three metric tons).

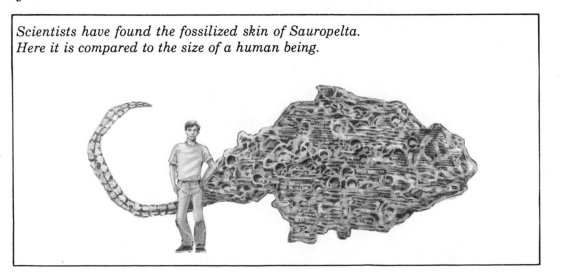

*Scientists have found the fossilized skin of Sauropelta. Here it is compared to the size of a human being.*

# Ceratopsians

The word *ceratopsians* means "horned faces." These ornithischian dinosaurs had horns or bony sections on their noses and foreheads. They also had hard, bony frills at the backs of their heads. These frills often covered their necks.

## Protoceratops (Pro-toe-SAIR-uh-tops)

*Protoceratops* means "first horned face." This is the earliest known horned dinosaur and may have been the ancestor of many later horned types. Protoceratops was only six feet (under two meters) long and weighed less than most other ceratopsians.

Protoceratops had an extremely large head with a small bony frill behind it. This stretched from the skull and had very powerful jaw muscles attached to it. This bony frill may have protected the creature's neck and shoulders.

*Protoceratops*

## Nests

Protoceratops' nests, discovered in the Mongolian desert, showed how the dinosaurs laid their eggs. Females made holes in the sand, then laid their eggs in a circle. The eggs were covered with sand so that they would stay warm and eventually hatch. Scientists do not know if Protoceratops took any further interest in the eggs after they had been laid.

The fossils found in these Protoceratops' nests showed that the potato-shaped eggs were about six inches (fifteen centimeters) long. The shells of these fossilized eggs were rough and wrinkly. The discovery of groups of nests made scientists realize that these dinosaurs lived in colonies.

*Baby Protoceratops hatching.*

## Triceratops (Try-SAIR-ah-tops)

*Triceratops* means "three-horned face." As its name suggests, this dinosaur had three horns. It was nearly thirty feet (nine meters) long and almost ten feet (three meters) high. It had thick legs to support its heavy body of about six tons (about five and a half metric tons).

From the many skulls that have been found, scientists know that this creature's head was almost one-fourth as long as its whole body. Triceratops had a moderately sized frill behind its head. The back of the frill had a number of bony lumps on it. Its beaklike mouth enabled it to feed on plants.

*Triceratops*

The horns of Triceratops were long and deadly. There was one about three feet (one meter) long over each eye, and a short, thick horn above its nose. Although Triceratops was a plant-eater, its horns were probably used to challenge rivals and to defend itself. Fossil skulls have been found with marks on them made by fights with other Triceratops.

*Triceratops defending itself against an attacking Tyrannosaurus.*

# LIFE IN THE SEAS

There were several kinds of marine and flying reptiles during the Age of the Dinosaurs. However, it is important to note that these were not dinosaurs.

## Ichthyosaurs (IK-thee-oh-SORZ)

These "fish lizards" looked and moved very much like our modern dolphins and porpoises. They were streamlined for fast swimming, with four smooth fins like flippers. Most ichthyosaurs were about ten to thirty feet (three to nine meters) long, although one fossil found in Nevada was about fifty feet (fifteen meters) long. Many well-preserved ichthyosaur fossils have helped scientists learn a lot about these sea creatures.

*Ichthyosaur*

**Nothosaurs** (NO-tho-sorz)
These creatures lived during the Triassic Period, 215 million years ago. They grew to about thirteen feet (four meters) in length and had a long skull with pointed teeth. Nothosaurs may have been able to move up on land and come ashore to have their young.

*Nothosaur*

**Plesiosaurs** (PLEE-zee-uh-sorz)
These fish-eating creatures with flippers lived in the oceans of the Mesozoic Era. The two kinds of plesiosaurs were pliosauroids (PLY-uh-SORE-oyds) and plesiosauroids (PLEE-zee-uh-SORE-oyds). Pliosauroids were probably like our modern whales, but with short necks and large heads. Plesiosauroids had long necks, small heads, and barrel-shaped bodies. They looked like the sea serpents of legends. Elasmosaurus (Ee-LAZ-muh-SORE-us) was a plesiosauroid. Fossils show that it grew to over forty-two feet (thirteen meters) in length.

# LIFE IN THE AIR

During the Late Triassic Period, more than 200 million years ago, the first pterosaurs ("winged lizards") began to use their leathery, batlike wings to fly or glide. They probably used rising air currents or breezes to get off the ground.

Some of these creatures were as small as sparrows. Others had a wingspan of almost fifty feet (fifteen meters).

### Pterodactyls (Ter-uh-DAK-tilz)
The name *pterodactyl* means "wing finger," because each wing was supported by a single extended fourth finger. A fossil of one of these creatures discovered in 1970 showed fine imprints of body fur. Pterodactyls fed off plankton or fish from the sea.

*Pterodactyl*

## Rhamphorhynchus (Ram-foh-RINK-us)

Rhamphorhynchus was a reptile eighteen inches (forty-six centimeters) long, with a wingspan four feet (one and a quarter meters) long. It had a toothed beak and a long tail ending in a flap like a boat's rudder for steering. Its diet consisted mainly of fish, but a large prehistoric dragonfly made a nice treat now and then.

*Rhamphorhynchus*

## Quetzalcoatlus (Ket-sol-koh-AT-lus)

This animal was the largest flying reptile. It had the wingspan of a World War II fighter plane – between thirty-six feet and fifty feet (eleven and fifteen meters) across. Scientists have been baffled as to how such large creatures launched themselves into the air. They could not have taken off from the ground under their own power. It seems more likely that they relied on strong updrafts of air to give them lift.

## Pteranodon (Ter-AN-o-don)

This fish-eating animal had a wingspan of twenty-seven feet (eight meters), and may have used its wings to glide on the winds blowing up the sides of sea cliffs. Its long head crest may have served as a rudder. Pteranodon fossils have been found in the United States and Japan.

*Pteranodon*

## Archaeopteryx (Ar-kee-OP-ter-ix)

*Archaeopteryx* means "ancient wing." Most scientists believe that these creatures were the world's first birds. They were not pterosaurs. Fossils show that Archaeopteryx had feathers on each wing, plus feathers on its body and tail. The first feathers may have developed from fringed scales. These Jurassic birds were about three feet (one meter) long. They could not fly very well, but achieved short flights by running into a headwind and jumping into the air. They may have used their sharp claws for climbing trees, and they could have glided back to the ground.

*Archaeopteryx*

# DEATH OF THE DINOSAURS

After ruling the earth for more than 140 million years, dinosaurs died out. About sixty-six million years ago, something happened that killed them all.

Some scientists think it happened in a comparatively short time, while others say the extinction was very gradual.

*Stegoceras*

There are many theories about the dinosaurs' death. Perhaps the meat-eaters ate up all the plant-eaters and were left without any other food.

Or maybe the huge creatures were too large to move or breed properly. Germs may have killed them, or they could have died from eating new types of flowering plants. Small mammals may have eaten their eggs.

None of these explanations seems very likely, though. The dinosaurs were well-developed creatures, able to cope with life as well as any other animal. These theories ignore that fact. They do not explain why so many other animals died at about the same time.

*Did small mammals eat the dinosaurs' eggs?*

# CHANGING WORLD OF THE DINOSAURS

Because these explanations did not satisfy scientists, experts have come up with new ideas.

## Cosmic Rays and Radiation

Some experts argue that cosmic rays from an exploding star could have killed the dinosaurs. Or changes in the earth's magnetic field may have allowed deadly radiation to pour in, destroying many forms of animal life.

*Dinosaurs such as boneheads, carnosaurs, and ceratopsians panic before the terrible force of an exploding star.*

## Environmental Changes

Other scientists argue that as the great land mass split up, some of the continents gradually drifted toward the icy poles. The resulting ice age would have killed off the dinosaurs because they would not have been able to stay warm enough.

Such changes in the environment and climate often take place slowly, over millions of years. But scientists think that the dinosaurs died out more suddenly. The key to this mystery may lie in another explanation.

*Dryptosaurus*

## The Greenhouse Effect

By 1980, scientists developed a new explanation for why the dinosaurs were suddenly killed off. Scientists who study the earth, called geologists (jee-OL-uh-jists), suggested that about sixty-six million years ago a lump of rock from a falling star or planet streaked in from space and crashed into the earth. This huge rock may have been six miles (ten kilometers) across, so it would have made an enormous impact.

If this theory is correct, great clouds of dust and moisture were thrown up into the atmosphere, and the skies were dark for months or even years. Because the sun's rays were blocked out, the earth grew cold very quickly, and an ice age may have occurred. This would have destroyed the plant life, leading to the death of plant-eating dinosaurs and eventually to the starvation of meat-eaters.

As the dust clouds gradually began to clear, they allowed the sun's rays to filter through. But the dust clouds also trapped the rays so that they could not escape. This "greenhouse effect" caused the earth to heat up quickly and become stifling. It is likely that the polar ice masses thawed and flooding occurred. Any dinosaurs that survived the ice age may have died by overheating or drowning.

# DISCOVERING THE DINOSAURS

Everything we know about dinosaurs comes from their fossils. Fossils are the remains or traces of dead animals and plants from long ago. Luckily, scientists have a rich supply of dinosaur fossils to study. Dinosaur bones have been discovered on every continent.

It's not surprising that dinosaurs have been found in so many different parts of the world. As we have seen, the world did not look as it does today during the early days of the dinosaurs (see page 10). At that time, dinosaurs were able to reach every corner of the earth. Then Pangaea broke up into two huge continents. All the northern lands were joined together in a continent called Laurasia (Lor-AY-Shah). The southern lands were once the supercontinent of Gondwanaland (Gond-WAH-nuh-land).

About sixty-six million years ago, the Mesozoic Era ended and the Cenozoic (Sen-uh-ZOH-ik) Era began. The continents continued to drift apart. North America was separated from Europe, and South America and Australia from Antarctica. Different kinds of animal life began to appear, but none as widespread as the early dinosaurs.

## First Finds

Dinosaur bones have been on earth for millions of years. But even as recently as 300 years ago, when some of the first fossils were found, no one knew what they were. Only since the early 1800s have scientists come to understand how fossils were formed and what information lies within them.

## Reading Fossils

Discoveries of the fossils of plants and other forms of life tell us what the world of the dinosaurs was like. Scientists who study fossils are called paleontologists (pay-lee-on-TOL-oh-jists). Paleontologists are able to "read" fossils, much like a book. They can draw a picture of what dinosaurs ate, how they lived and died, and what they looked like.

*Fossils*

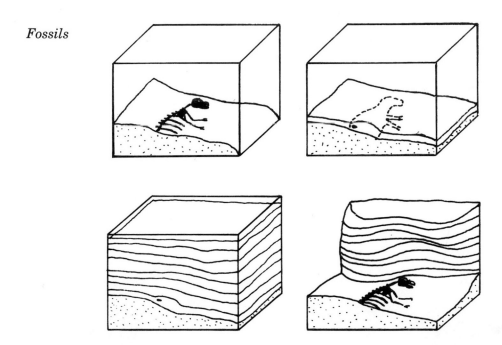

*Fossils occur when the remains of a dinosaur, in this case its bones (top left), become covered with mud (top right). Over millions of years the layers of mud turn to rock (bottom left) and only when that rock is worn away or removed is the fossil exposed (bottom right).*

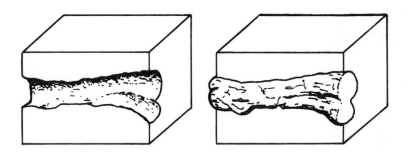

*What is left over when the rock is removed is either a fossil impression of the bone that was embedded in rock (left), or an actual fossil bone (right).*

# HOW DINOSAURS BECAME FOSSILIZED

These five pictures give a clearer idea of how a dinosaur becomes fossilized.

1. A drowned sauropod sinks to the bottom of a lake.

2. Mud settles on the lake bed and buries the body.

3. The flesh rots away. Minerals seep into the bones and turn them partly to stone.

4. Movements of the earth's crust during earthquakes can push the fossil near the surface.

5. Wind, rain, and floods often wash away rock and expose the fossil.

1.

4.
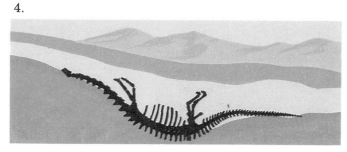

2.

5.

3.

## Molds and Casts

A fossil mold is produced when a bone decays and leaves its shape in the rock. If the bone shape becomes filled with minerals, the result is a fossil cast.

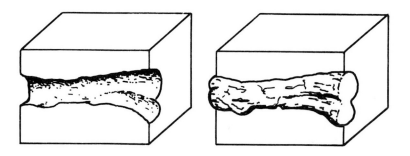

## Kinds of Fossils

1. Footprints in mud can turn into fossils if the mud turns into rock before water washes the prints away.

2. Skin and hide can leave fossilized molds.

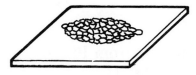

3. Fossil dinosaur eggs have also survived.

# PIONEERS IN DISCOVERY
## Early American Finds

### Casper Wistar

In 1787, an anatomist (person who studies the shape and structure of living things) named Casper Wistar reported the discovery of a gigantic bone in Philadelphia. It was probably a thighbone from a duck-billed dinosaur. Sadly, this has since been lost.

### Pliny Moody

Later, in 1802, a Massachusetts college student named Pliny Moody found tracks of huge "birds" while plowing his father's field. These were imprinted in the sandstone near his home. Not until the 1860s did people realize that these were the footprints of early dinosaurs.

### Joseph Leidy

Joseph Leidy, an anatomist from Philadelphia, named the first American dinosaurs in 1856. One was a duck-billed plant-eater, which he named Trachodon (TRAK-oh-don), or "rough tooth." The other was a small flesh-eater, which he named Deinodon (DINE-no-don), or "terror tooth." They were known only from teeth found two years before in Montana. Then, in 1858, Leidy named the remains of another duck-billed dinosaur, calling it Hadrosaurus ("bulky lizard"). The worldwide hunt for dinosaurs had begun.

# British Discoveries

### Robert Plot

More than 300 years ago, an English museum keeper, Robert Plot, found the thighbone of a Megalosaurus. He was convinced that it came from a human giant.

### Mary Ann Mantell

During a walk down a country lane in 1822, Mary Ann Mantell found some Iguanodon teeth among some road builder's stones. Her husband, Dr. Gideon Mantell, published the first account of the plant-eating dinosaur.

### William Buckland

William Buckland described the sharp-fanged, flesh-eating Megalosaurus in 1824. Megalosaurus was the first dinosaur to be scientifically named and described.

# FAMOUS FOSSIL HUNTERS AND THEIR FINDS

The early finds of dinosaur remains fired the imaginations of American fossil hunters. During the 1870s, two wealthy American scientists began the longest dinosaur quest in the United States up to that time. Othniel Charles Marsh and Edward Drinker Cope each hired teams of fossil hunters whose finds amazed the world. The fossils they found showed the world just how huge, plentiful, and varied some of the groups of dinosaurs had been.

*Marsh*   *Cope*

## Rivalry

Marsh and Cope were so jealous of each other that each team tried to keep their finds a secret. So fierce was the competition that the two teams came to blows more than once.

## The Race

The hunt became a race to find the best fossil beds. In 1877, Marsh's team discovered bones near Morrison, Colorado. Meanwhile, near Canon City, south of Morrison, Cope's team was digging up huge bones farther along in the same rock formation.

*Scientists are still digging fossils out of the sites Marsh and Cope discovered.*

## Como Bluff

Both of the original sites of Marsh and Cope were dwarfed by Como Bluff, a ridge in southern Wyoming. It was here that Marsh's team found mighty fossil bones, thickly clustered over seven miles (about eleven kilometers). Marsh and his crew spent years mining quarries to extract the dinosaur bones, while discouraging Cope's attempts to do the same.

## New Species

Both men achieved enormous success. Between them they found 136 new species of American dinosaurs. Before they started searching, only nine dinosaur species were known in the United States.

## Othniel Charles Marsh (1831-1899)

Four of his best-known discoveries are shown here:

*Diplodocus*          *Allosaurus*          *Stegosaurus*          *Triceratops*

## Edward Drinker Cope (1840-1897)

Here are three of his best-known discoveries:

*Camarasaurus*          *Monoclonius*          *Coelophysis*

# MORE DISCOVERIES IN NORTH AMERICA

## The United States

Collectors working for museums have added greatly to the earlier discoveries of Marsh and Cope. The United States has proved to be a rich source of dinosaur fossils from the Triassic, Jurassic, and Cretaceous Periods.

## Fossil Cabin

Between 1878 and 1905, a team from the American Museum of Natural History discovered tons of fossils from various sites in Wyoming. One of these was the famous Bone Cabin Quarry, named after a cabin there built entirely of dinosaur bones.

## Dinosaur Menagerie

In 1909, Earl Douglass, working for Pittsburgh's Carnegie Museum, began digging up a menagerie (collection of animals) of Jurassic dinosaurs. He took them from Carnegie quarry, carved in rock east of Vernal, Utah. This rich source of fossils is now Dinosaur National Monument.

*Earl Douglass*

## Recent North American Ideas

Since the 1960s, the work of John Ostrom, Peter Galton, Robert Bakker, and others has greatly increased our knowledge of Jurassic and Cretaceous dinosaurs. These individuals have given us new ideas that have helped change the way we think about dinosaurs.

## Canada

At the end of the 1880s, a fossil "rush" began in Canada after Joseph Burr Tyrrell had made a major discovery there. Its aim was to find the skeletons of hundreds of dinosaurs that lived seventy-six to sixty-six million years ago on what were then warm, wooded, swampy plains between the Rocky Mountains and an inland sea.

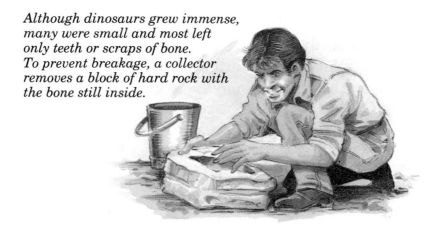

*Although dinosaurs grew immense, many were small and most left only teeth or scraps of bone. To prevent breakage, a collector removes a block of hard rock with the bone still inside.*

## Red Deer River

In 1910, Barnum Brown began collecting many fossil bones from around the Red Deer River in Alberta. Since then, the Red Deer River has been the site of various expeditions. These have resulted in a rich harvest of Late Cretaceous duckbills, horned dinosaurs, and carnosaurs.

## Fossilized Herds

More recently, many finds have come from Dinosaur Provincial Park, bordering the Red Deer River. In the late 1970s and early 1980s, scientists found fossil beds so rich that they could hardly avoid stepping on the bones of herds of horned dinosaurs.

## A Pickled Dinosaur?

Even richer finds may come from farther north of the Red Deer River. Here, Early Cretaceous tree leaves are found pickled (preserved in a liquid solution) by Alberta's oily tar sands. Perhaps one day scientists may find pickled dinosaur remains as well.

# DISCOVERIES IN EUROPE

Ever since the discovery of dinosaur fossils in England (see page 79), collectors have scoured Europe's Mesozoic rocks for more.

## Germany

Rocks beneath southwest Germany's rolling woods and fertile farmland have yielded exciting discoveries of early dinosaurs. By 1837, paleontologist Hermann von Meyer had already described Plateosaurus, a big plant-eater that roamed around Triassic Germany more than 200 million years ago. Later, in 1910, more Plateosaurus bones were found in a southern German quarry. According to one theory, the animals may have died on a long desert trek in search of food.

Also in southern Germany, the actual impression of the feathers of Archaeopteryx was first found in 1860. Hermann von Meyer studied the fossil and named it.

**GERMANY**

## Britain

Many different kinds of dinosaurs roamed southern Britain in Early Cretaceous times. Rocks in the area contain the remains of Iguanodons, boneheads, armored dinosaurs, and other ornithischians; ferocious meat-eaters such as Megalosaurus; and huge plant-eating sauropods. These roamed about in a large, marshy area that in prehistoric times sprawled across to France and Belgium. That marshy area is now covered by the English Channel.

## Belgium and France

In 1878, Belgian coal miners made an exciting find. Working 1,056 feet (322 meters) below the surface, they found the fossilized bodies of more than thirty Iguanodons that had fallen down a steep ravine and died. Another fascinating find was the large fossil eggs unearthed in France. They are among the largest dinosaur eggs ever found.

**EUROPE**

# DISCOVERIES IN OTHER PARTS OF THE WORLD

## Asia

The great inland basins of southern Mongolia have proved to be among the richest dinosaur boneyards anywhere. The first expedition was organized by the American Museum of Natural History in 1922. Scientists drove hundreds of miles in cars and trucks into the Gobi Desert. Their supplies were brought in by seventy-five camels. Mongolia has been one of the world's richest treasuries of Late Cretaceous dinosaurs.

## China

Most of the discoveries here have been made since the 1950s. Discoveries include the largest duckbill known, very long-necked sauropods, and Asian plated dinosaurs.

## India

In 1960, scientists found the remains of one of the earliest known sauropods. Dinosaur remains are not so plentiful here and are mainly of the Late Cretaceous Period.

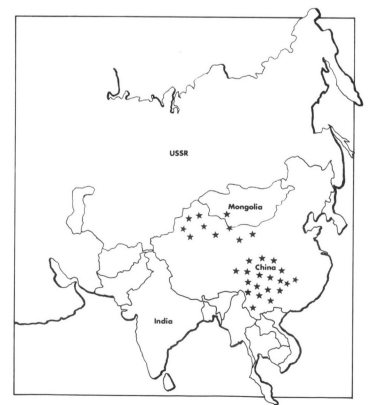

ASIA

## Africa

Africa was the home of many early dinosaurs. German expeditions between 1909 and 1912 unearthed the famous "bone beds" in what is now Tanzania. Collectors shipped 1,000 boxes of fossils to Germany, totaling 250 tons (228 metric tons).

## South America

Up until 1979, most of the discoveries on this continent were of Late Cretaceous fossils, with one or two Jurassic and Triassic remains. Recent finds include duckbills, which were once unknown in the Southern Hemisphere. Some scientists think that South America is where dinosaur life began.

## Australia and the South Pacific

Until the 1980s, most finds in this part of the world had been accidental. Only one Triassic and one Jurassic migrant had been discovered. Now scientists know of a greater variety of dinosaurs from finds in this region. In 1980, the first New Zealand dinosaur was discovered – a flesh-eater about thirteen feet (four meters) long.

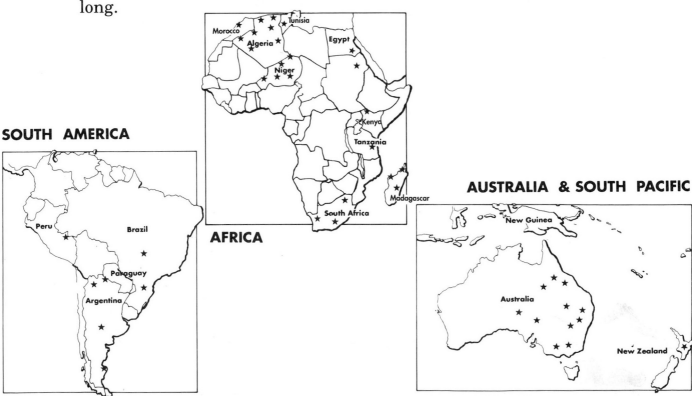

# HOW FOSSILS ARE PRESERVED

Digging up a dinosaur fossil is just the start. Fossil hunters must then take it to a museum where experts can study it in workshops and laboratories.

The fossil hunters harden crumbling bones with a special paint or spray. Plaster or polystyrene foam jackets may be used to help protect bones for carrying them to a museum.

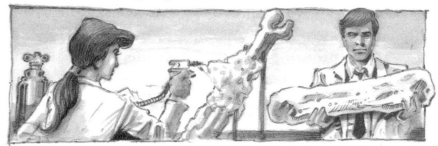

Inside the museum, the packaging is removed from the bones. Technicians may spend months trimming off stone still clinging to fossils. They use hammers, chisels, and even dentists' drills. Casts of the bones are often used to reconstruct the skeletons. This is because the actual bones are too valuable, brittle, or heavy.

## Rebuilding

Once the bones are clean, scientists try to work out just how they all fit together. Technicians then rebuild the whole skeleton. Metal braces and clamps help to pose the skeleton as the living animal once stood.

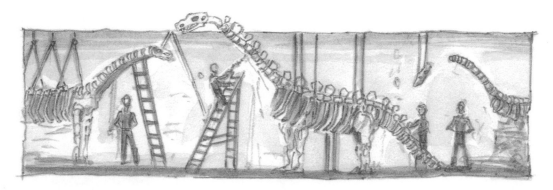

*Museum workers rebuilding a giant skeleton.*

## On Display

After perhaps years of work by many people, the fossil dinosaur is ready for display.

Even during display, paleontologists will study its bones. The skull of the fossil dinosaur tells them what kind of eyes, nose, teeth, and brain the creature had. These are all clues as to how well a dinosaur could think, see, and smell, and also to what kind of food it ate. Leg bones show whether it walked or ran. Marks on bones left by muscles can even give an idea of the leg's actual shape and size.

*A completed skeleton on display.*

New dinosaur fossils are discovered all the time. As scientists continue to study the clues from the past, we are sure to learn more about these strange, mysterious creatures from millions of years ago.

# DINOSAUR DISPLAYS IN THE UNITED STATES

There are many places in the United States where bones, skulls, and even whole skeletons of dinosaurs can be viewed. Listed below are details of some of the museums that have displays, and the specific dinosaurs that are on show.

*Spectators look on as a technician carefully chisels away at the fossil-rich rock.*

**Jensen, Utah:** Dinosaur National Monument.
These 206,000 acres (83,368 hectares) of fossil-rich canyons include a covered Quarry Visitor Center where spectators view technicians revealing 2000 dinosaur bones embedded in this former Carnegie Quarry. Late Jurassic fossils found here include: the carnosaurs *Allosaurus* and *Ceratosaurus*; the sauropods *Apatosaurus*, *Camarasaurus*, and *Diplodocus*; the ornithopods *Camptosaurus* and *Dryosaurus*; and the plated *Stegosaurus*, of which the smallest known specimen is on display.

**New York City, New York:** American Museum of Natural History. This has the world's largest dinosaur collection, with a wealth of skeletons and skulls of North American dinosaurs and also fossil tracks, skin impressions, and eggs. There are complete skeletons of the following dinosaurs: the coelurosaurs *Coelophysis*, and *Struthiomimus*; the carnosaurs *Albertosaurus*, *Allosaurus*, and *Tyrannosaurus*; the prosauropod *Plateosaurus*; the sauropod *Apatosaurus*; the ornithopods *Camptosaurus*, *Corythosaurus*, *Lambeosaurus (young)*, and *Saurolophus*; the plated dinosaur *Stegosaurus*; the armored dinosaur *Panoplosaurus*; and the horned dinosaurs *Monoclonius*, *Protoceratops*, *Styracosaurus*, and *Triceratops*.

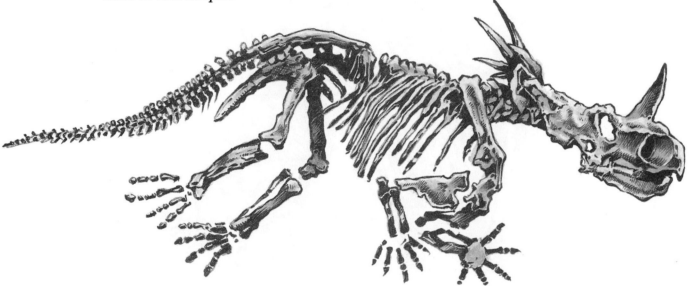

*Skeleton of Styracosaurus*

**New Haven, Connecticut:** Peabody Museum of Natural History, Yale University.
Pioneered by Othniel Charles Marsh, this museum features many important types of specimens. It includes an *Allosaurus (Antrodemus)* skull; skeletons of the sauropods *Apatosaurus* and *Camarasaurus*; skeletons of the ornithopods *Camptosaurus* and *Anatosaurus*; skeletons of *Stegosaurus* and *Monoclonius*; skulls of the horned dinosaur *Triceratops*; and various casts.

**Washington, DC:** National Museum of Natural History, Smithsonian Institution.

This has a fine collection of displayed skeletons, and stores many types of specimens.  The renovated Dinosaur Hall reopened in 1981.  National Museum specimens include the following (all from  North America): the carnosaurs *Albertosaurus*, *Allosaurus*, and *Tyrannosaurus*; the sauropods *Camarasaurus* and *Diplodocus*; the ornithopods *Camptosaurus* and *Corythosaurus*; *Stegosaurus*; and the horned *Triceratops*.

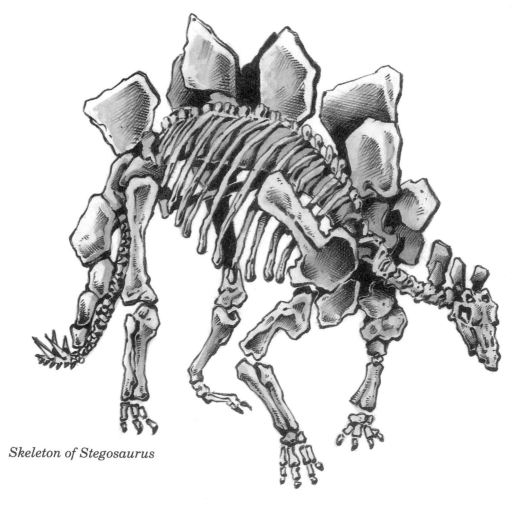

*Skeleton of Stegosaurus*

**Los Angeles, California**: Los Angeles County Museum of Natural History.

Displays include skeletons of an *Allosaurus* as if attacking a *Camptosaurus*; and the duckbill *Corythosaurus*. There are also skulls of *Tyrannosaurus* (finely preserved) and *Parasaurolophus*.

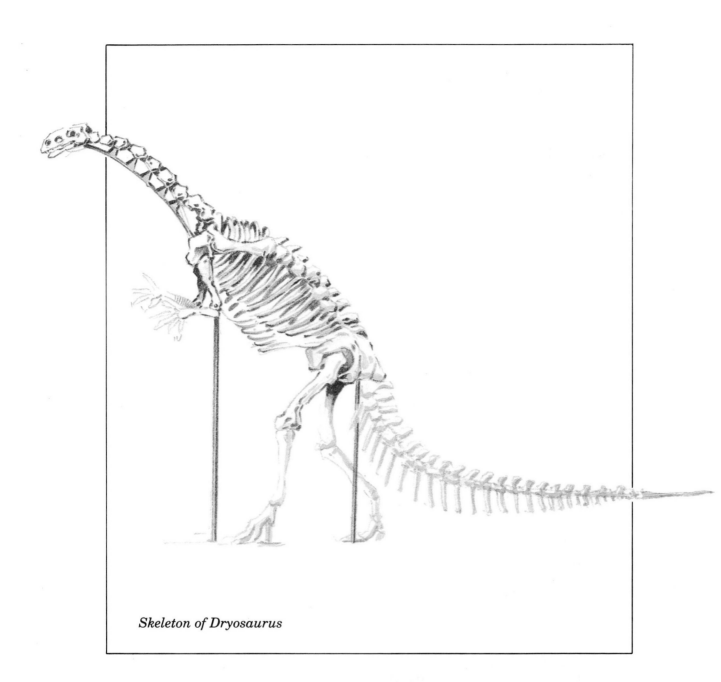

Skeleton of Dryosaurus

**Pittsburgh, Pennsylvania:** Carnegie Museum of Natural History. The Mesozoic Hall has some of the world's best specimens of Late Jurassic and Cretaceous dinosaurs, with 10 skeletons: the carnosaurs *Allosaurus* and *Tyrannosaurus*; the sauropods *Apatosaurus*, *Camarasaurus*, and *Diplodocus*; the ornithopods *Camptosaurus*, *Corythosaurus*, and *Dryosaurus*; the horned dinosaur *Protoceratops*; and the plated *Stegosaurus*. There are also five skulls, plaster casts, and scores of stored bones.